AF348477

Ironton Park

Wilson Mesa

WESTERN REFLECTIONS
PUBLISHING COMPANY

ISBN 1-890437-97-2

Library of Congress Number: 2003113338

For more information on
Bob DeJulio, go to:
www.pro-techs.net/dejulio

Cover and Text Design by Susan Smilanic, SJS Design
Text and captions by P. David Smith

First Edition
Printed in China

Western Reflections Publishing Co.
219 Main Street
Montrose, CO 81401
www.westernreflectionspub.com

Cloud Burst

1990s

Watercolor.

The Kid

1980s

Watercolor.

DEJULIO.
"THE BIG BLUE"

True Grit

2000
Bob painted the sign on
the window from this set
in the movie *True Grit*.

Watercolor.

Robert James DeJulio was born at Old St. Luke's Hospital in Montrose, Colorado, on January 22, 1931, but his heart lives in the 1890s in the middle of the majestic San Juan Mountains. The DeJulio family has lived in southwest Colorado for well over a hundred years, and "Bob," as he is known to everyone in Montrose, has spent much of his life listening to any "old-timer" who was willing to talk about the way it was at the end of the nineteenth century and the beginning of the twentieth. It is a trait that is much more common for an author/historian than an artist, but Bob is a very special type of artist — one who recreates history for the modern eye to visually enjoy.

Bob DeJulio can take historic scenes that were never photographed and bring them to life through visualizing and then painting the stories and tales of the pioneers — all of whom are now gone but many of whom spent countless hours being primed by Bob for the details of a way of life that will forever remain frozen in time because of the paintings of Bob DeJulio. Bob is a master of using the brush and canvas to capture the true Old West — accurate to every detail, although Bob's paintings also leave plenty of room for the viewers to fill in their own interpretations.

Bob was born and raised on a farm that stood near the present-day Black Canyon Golf Course. He still lives on a small part of the farm owned by his father, James DeJulio. His real last name was DiGulio, as there is no "J" in the Italian alphabet, but as with so many hard to pronounce foreign names, his last name was "Americanized" into DeJulio (later he even obtained a registered trademark on the name DeJulio). He went to school in Montrose, then started work at the local JC Penney store, and later transferred to the big city – Colorado Springs – in 1951. Bob had no formal art training, but had a real knack for graphic or commercial art. The people that he worked with also strongly encouraged him to pursue his art. He had enjoyed drawing from an early age, but there were no art classes given in the schools at that time. Later he did advertising and display work for Penney.

He started painting seriously in Colorado Springs, but his art has always been secondary to a "paying job." In 1955 he married Wanda F. Vogel, who was originally from Kansas, but worked under him at the JC Penney in Colorado Springs. They were married for forty-seven years until Wanda passed away in 2002. Bob refers to Wanda as "his harshest critic" but has great respect for her opinion about his art. He states that she had an uncanny way about knowing how his work would be received. Eventually they had two children, Paul (who now works for the Highway Department in Gypsum, Colorado) and Ben (who is a builder in Silverthorne, Colorado). Between the two sons, Bob and Wanda had eight grandchildren.

When Bob started painting in earnest in 1951, he used mainly oils and most of the paintings that he intended to sell were of Navajo Indians and Navajoland (even though he had only been there a few times). He also painted scenes that included his family members and friends (like the one of his grandparents, Felix and Louise Keep, and Louie and Mary DiCamillo done in 1951 and found in this book). Many of the paintings were from memory or he recreated scenes from before his time that were told to him. He enjoyed being in Colorado Springs, which was an art colony at the time that equaled Taos. He liked to browse around the local galleries and patterned his art after what he saw (it was what drew him to the Navajo scenes). He especially liked the paintings of Greg Bartlett and Sharp, who were a part of the famous "Taos Ten" and all of whom were painters that inspired Bob. However it was a time when abstract art was in and realism was out, and Bob preferred for his work to have a more realistic tone. Unfortunately his work did not sell well. As Bob puts it, "people with money didn't buy my work, but those without money seemed to like it." In 1958 he began doing landscapes of the Old West, which was great practice for the backgrounds of many of his future paintings. Now he considers his landscapes to be purely secondary.

Bob and Wanda moved back to Montrose in 1958, where he was hired by a sign company, then worked for himself as a sign painter, and then got a job with Colorado Ute for fourteen years doing photography and drawing maps and charts. He was doing commercial art – lots of scenes of power lines - but he also did paintings and drawings for the monthly magazines and work for the company's board meetings. He learned a lot about the history of Ames – the first commercially generated alternating current in the United States and located just outside Telluride. He wrote stories about the early days of electricity and illustrated them with his art. Bob enjoyed his time at Colorado Ute, but

unfortunately they had an "Enron" type closing and he lost his pension.

As stated earlier, Wanda was his harshest critic, but she also seemed to have an uncanny sense of what would sell. She was the one that suggested that he start painting historical scenes. "What are you painting Indians for? You don't know anything about them. Paint what you know about," she said.

A short time later Bob began painting in watercolors. Fritz Hanna, who owned the Red Barn at the time, had bought several pieces of his work, but asked Bob if he could do something in a watercolor. Everyone who saw his work at the Red Barn seemed to love it and asked him to do more. He felt he had finally found his niche. Fritz still has Bob's first watercolor – a street scene in Telluride. Bob relates, almost with sadness, that his early paintings had lots of detail. Over the next twenty years Bob's watercolors would become looser and looser, leaving much more to the viewers imagination. Some people seem to like the looser style better (Bob sure does), but he also realizes that when he does a commissioned work that there better be a lot of detail in it. So Bob still paints with and without a great deal of detail.

Bob started doing tempera-India ink resist at the same time as he started doing watercolors. He is very proud of his tempera-India ink resist paintings as they are very hard to do and are fast becoming a lost art. It is a process where the painting is done in tempera on watercolor paper. The part that will eventually become black ink is left blank, and then the painting is covered with black ink, which sticks only to the part left blank. Finally the whole painting is soaked in water for a few minutes.

Because of Wanda, Bob's painting began to head towards the historical. He had relatives that were farmers, railroad workers, and miners near the turn of the century. His grandfather had come to the United States in 1890 from Roccocarominico, Italy, (which is located in the mountains of central Italy) and his first job was to work with Otto Mears on the construction of the Rio Grande Southern Railroad from Ridgway to Durango. Later he became a section boss at Matterhorn, a small station near Trout Lake. Bob's father was born in Telluride and later worked in the mines near Rico. Bob's uncles, Carl and Rocco, homesteaded and farmed in the Dallas Divide area. Bob had his own experiences of growing up on a farm near Montrose. Yet this wasn't enough historical information for Bob.

Bob does meticulous research for most of his paintings. He has looked at a lot of old photographs, but most of the actual input for his drawings comes from stories. He's listened to hundreds if not thousands of stories told by old timers. He credits Tuffy Flor in Ouray for a lot of his information about what it was like to grow up in the mountains near the turn of the century. He spent a lot of time with Ben Gray learning about ranching and the life of a cowboy. Dick Spencer of the *Western Horseman* magazine also gave him a lot of good, detailed, constructive criticism. Bob would let them look at his paintings and tell him what was wrong – "The saddle is wrong" or "The slickers wouldn't look like that."

Bob says that the miners themselves didn't have much to say. A lot of what he learned was from his relatives, or observation, or from Tuffy Flor, who wasn't a miner himself. Bob's uncles mined in Rico and Telluride and had a lot of good stories to tell about the mines and miners. Interestingly, Bob has only done one painting of mining in the Rico area as he didn't consider the landscapes in the vicinity to be as interesting as other parts of the San Juans. He also got a lot of information

from his uncle Paul DiCamillo who drove an ore wagon.

In 1953 Bob also spent many hours talking to an eighty-five year old stagecoach driver, Earl May, who ran the route from Cañon City to Victor. He told Bob that the drivers put ground up red chili peppers in their boots to irritate their toes and keep them from freezing. Earl May's wife bowled with Wanda, while Earl related to Bob many stories of early pioneers who were killed or shot. Another favorite friend was Harold David, who checked sheep permits high in the San Juans from the 1940s until the 1970s. Bob not only learned about the high country, but also was taken on a backcountry trip to many of the places that Harold had talked about. Bob met and talked to many of the sheepherders (all known personally by Harold), although many were Basque and could not speak English. Martin Echardt, who is one of the biggest sheepmen in Montrose and grazed his animals on Dallas Divide and in the San Juans in the summer, was another source of several stories. Frank Williams, who had a 5,000-acre ranch next to Marie Scott, also shared many sheepherding stories with Bob.

All of his time wasn't spent talking with people. Bob also spent a lot of

time in Johnny Johnson's old museum in Ouray looking closely at many of the objects that he included in his work, and he travels frequently to the high country to check out the background landscapes for his scenes. Just in the last two summers he went to Hurricane Basin to see the old Galconda boardinghouse which is being restored and visited the restored Sound Democrat Mill high above Animas Forks. He keeps photographs around for the scenery, but the people and animals usually come strictly out of his imagination.

Some of Bob's paintings are done on commission – a historical scene that a family wants to recreate yet doesn't have a photograph. Many of his paintings have become a family treasure, a reminder of days gone by, and many of these people have filled him in on details of how it was in the old days. Bob's own family supplies many of these stories and details, like his Aunt Elsie (married to his father's brother) who owned a hardware store in Telluride and was fairly well to do. They had their own private stagecoach, pulled by four white horses, and would bring presents to the family children in Montrose at Christmas time.

In the late 1960s Bob worked on the sets of *True Grit* and *How the West Was Won*.

2000
Since Bob was often in the Ophir area to see his family, he drew this scene from memory. The Silver Bell Mill is in the background.

Watercolor.

He literally worked on them — painting signs on buildings and doing artwork (like wood graining) on the sets themselves. He points out that Hollywood really did try to be authentic on their sets. He met John Wayne, Gregory Peck, and many other famous actresses and actors. Bob has continued this tradition by painting many of the sets for the Magic Circle Players (he did all of *The Sound Of Music* set) but he says that it has become just too big a job as he has gotten older. He still does occasional work on a float or for backgrounds at the museums.

Because of his love of art (but also because of the failure of his pension system) Bob continued to work, for ten years for the Best Sign Systems, until he just recently retired. He says that he still spends a great deal of his time doing volunteer work and the rest is spent teaching or painting. That is something Bob has done all his life. He points out that 98% of all painters have to work a "real" job — that only 2% can make a living from their art alone. He has become a prominent member of the local art community and is often called on for advice. He often teaches a continuing education class for Mesa College and at other seminars. But Bob himself never stops learning. He is always interested in new techniques or in a new story about the Old West.

Bob cannot begin to count the number of paintings that he has done over the more than fifty years that he has been painting. Many of them were not photographed by him and many of the originals have been resold or were moved with their families out of the area. This book concentrates heavily on ones that Bob has attached a special meaning to — some of which he still has in his house. Yet any observant Montrose citizen can see his paintings daily. They hang on the walls of restaurants, banks, and many other businesses throughout the town. He still continues to paint on a regular basis, sometimes getting carried away and working until 2:00 a.m. There are still many subjects that he has not yet painted. Hopefully, for our sake, he will find the time to do them.

Perhaps the best thing that can be said about Bob is that he is truly a really nice person. He is generous beyond fault — always willing to help others, always willing to donate a painting to a charitable cause. Bob lives a modest life and is a modest man, but what he has accomplished is much more important than much of that done by people with a lot of money or a lot of ambition. He is undoubtedly the senior statesman of the Montrose, perhaps even the southwestern Colorado, art community; but he would never say so, or even think such a thing.

As we talked of doing this book Bob would always say — "Well you just do what you think best, Dave." He made it clear that it was more important what I thought and what I liked. He does the same thing with his painting. The primary purpose is always to please his audience. He is an incredibly talented man, but he still acts as if he is surprised that anyone likes his work. People constantly ask him to do prints of his work or to paint their favorite scene from the past. I have no doubt that if a poll was taken and the people of Montrose were asked who their favorite artist was, that Bob DeJulio would be at the top of the list. I also have no doubt if the people of Montrose were asked who their favorite person was, that Bob DeJulio would also be at the top of the list, for Bob is a truly loving, caring man. No person could do better than to be able to say, "Bob DeJulio is my friend."

P. David Smith

Publisher/Author

1980
The ore wagons are
coming down from the
Camp Bird Mine to Ouray
in a major snowstorm.

Tempera- India ink resist.

San Miguel Canyon

1992
This Rio Grande Southern
train is entering the
San Miguel Canyon
near Placerville.

Watercolor.

Twenty Below Zero

Early 1970s
Freighters had to
stop and build a fire in
order to warm up.

Watercolor.

Ute Mother and Child

Early 1960s
This painting was based
on a never published
black and white Bob
Gilmore photograph.
Bob researched the
colors carefully and
painted it soon after he
moved back to Montrose.

Oil.

1 9 5 0 s

1951
Bob's father and
aunt making lard at the
family ranch near the
present-day Black Canyon
Golf Course.

Oil.

1951
Bob often painted his family early in his career. Left to right are Pete Deltondo, Tony Keep, and Paul Dicamillo. All were farmers from Roccocarmonica, Italy.

Oil.

1950s
Bob painted this scene of what his grandparents (left) and Louie and Mary Dicamillo would have looked like during Prohibition. Note the beer bottle in his grandfather's hand.

Oil.

Mother and Child

1950s
A Navajo Madonna
scene in front of their
mud hogan.

Oil.

1960s

Tinkerbell

Early 1960s
This Indian boy's
name was Tinkerbell
and Bob painted him
near his home in
Monument Valley.

Oil.

Tinker's Mom

Early 1960s
Bob was concentrating
on Native American
subjects "like every one
else at the time," so he
spent some time in
Monument Valley.

Oil.

Desert Scene

Early 1960s
Bob did this scene
on commission for
Homer Puckett. It was
located near the Four
Corners area.

Oil.

1960s
Bob did this painting from memory. The wedding was at Carl DeJulio's home. Bob is the little boy on the right.

Watercolor.

Massorotti Ranch

1968
Bob painted this scene
for the owners of the
property. The ranch is
featured in the closing of
the movie *True Grit*.

Watercolor.

The Duke

1968
Bob did this painting of
John Wayne when he
was working on the set
of *True Grit*. He later did
many more portraits of
Wayne from memory.

Tempera- India ink resist.

1970s

1970
This was one of Bob's
first historical scenes from
the San Juans after he
switched to watercolors.
Tomboy Basin really does
look like this in May or
early June.

Watercolor.

Christmas in the Gunnison Valley

Late 1970s
Colorado Ute used this painting for their Christmas cover. It shows the great detail of some of Bob's earlier watercolors.

Watercolor.

Harnessing Up

1979
This scene could be anywhere. The horses are being readied for a days work.

Watercolor.

Flight for Life

1976
Bob likes this painting enough that he still owns it. It shows the near panic of the horses.

Tempera- India ink resist.

To Build A Fire

1970s
A scene during a cold
winter storm, high in
the San Juan Mountains.
Bob does a great job
of indicating the
strong wind.

Watercolor.

Savage Basin

1970s
This scene would have
been early in the Tomboy
Mine's history. The snow
piled up high here.

Watercolor.

Red Mountain Rain

Early 1970s
This is one of Bob's early
watercolors and he likes
the rain effect.

Watercolor.

Silverton Classic

1970s
This classic Silverton
house sits surrounded
by the high winter snows
with Kendall Mountain
in the background.
Evening comes early
this time of year.

Tempera- India ink resist.

Sunup at the Bachelor Mine

1970s
The ore wagon has
just been loaded at the
Bachelor Mine near
Ouray and the buildings
were recreated from
skeletal remains on
the property.

Watercolor.

Hitchin' Up

1979
A typical farming or
ranching scene from the
19th century, this time
from the Deep Creek
area off Last Dollar Road
near Telluride.

Tempera- India ink resist.

The Tomboy Mine

Early 1970s
Bob painted the backlit sunrise like it was an explosion coming from the mill.

Tempera- India ink resist.

Pack String From Savage Basin

1976
Supplies are being picked up from Columbia or San Miguel City as this scene is before there was a Telluride.

Watercolor.

The Surveyors

1979
Mining surveyors
are packing their
equipment in front
of the Pride of the
West Mill at Howardsville
near Silverton. The
tram brought ore from
the mine.

Tempera- India ink resist.

1979
Bob points out the
individual reins to each of
the six horses getting
ready to move out on an
early Silverton morning.

Watercolor.

Dusty Storm

1970s
The stagecoach was
coming from Gunnison.
Bob especially likes
the light in the clouds
in this work.

Watercolor.

1970s
The driver on the stage on the Million Dollar Highway is notified of an avalanche. He'll have to turn around!

Watercolor.

Silverton Main Street

1970s
Bob likes the way the yellows and reds really pop out in a tempera. They are much brighter than in a watercolor.

Tempera-India ink resist.

Phantom Canyon

1979
There is not room for the stage and the prospector to pass in this narrow gorge. Bob's friend Earl May actually drove this road in a Mud Wagon like this. Bob won a silver medal at the Denver Western Art Show with this work.

Watercolor.

1 9 8 0 s

1980s
The train is leaving
town headed east.
The depot is behind
the water tower. Bob
especially likes the play
of light in this painting.

Watercolor.

1980s
The north side of the
Telluride streets is the
sunniest as the buildings
face south. It is an
important consideration
in the winter.

Watercolor.

1980s
The town of Telluride
was the first in the United
States to have alternating
current electricity and
street lights like this
allowed work to continue
at night.

Watercolor.

The Revenue Mill

1980s
Bob was commissioned
to paint this scene for
Phil Trumbo. The
Revenue was located
above the Camp Bird
Mine near Ouray and
was one of the largest
and most profitable mills
in the United States.

Watercolor.

Out Before Winter

1980s
Bob imagined this prospector making a mad dash to get out of the mountain before the next big storm trapped him for months.

Watercolor.

Shadow of the Rio Grande

1980s
The Rio Grande Southern not only cast a shadow over the cowboys at the top of Dallas Divide, but the railroad's own days were numbered.

Watercolor.

Ophir Gold

1980s
Both the pack train and the railroad were important means of transportation around the famous Ophir Loop on the Rio Grande Southern. Bob's grandfather was a section man at Ophir.

Watercolor.

1980s
This mine was one of the first great discoveries in the San Juans, but its rich ore proved to be spotty.

Watercolor.

Cutting Barley on Wilson Mesa

1980s
There were many small farms on the mesas growing grains that were badly needed for the dairy cows and the horses of the era.

Watercolor.

1981
Today this is called Gold King Basin. Bob did the painting from a photo and gave the work to his son.

Watercolor.

1980s
Pack mules had to
be tied together
which could create
a large mess.

Oil.

Rain Storm Murphy Mine

1982
Painted for a Texas man,
the mine was located
out of Buena Vista
past Chalk Cliff.

Watercolor.

The Matterhorn

1981
Bob's friend Harold David took him into American Flats where they bumped into sheepherders. The scene could have been from a 100 years earlier.

Watercolor.

Chain the Wheels

Cowboys Bring Their Bootleg to Telluride

1980s
A small operator brings
his supply of bootleg
whiskey to Telluride to sell
in a back alley at night.

Watercolor.

The Toll Gate

Early 1980s
Otto Mears built his
tollhouse and tollgate
almost on top of Bear
Creek Falls near Ouray.

Watercolor.

Cimarron Elk

1980s
A scene from near the top of Owl Creek Pass near the Big Blue Wilderness area.

Watercolor.

The Big Blue

1980s
Bob painted this work with a pallet knife. Harold David, his two boys, Bob, and his son Paul spent a week in this wilderness area.

Acrylic.

·DE JULIO·
"BUTTON BOX"

Button Box

1980s
This painting represents
the typical Saturday
night entertainment
in the nineteenth century
for the local immigrants —
mainly Italian,
Swede, or Welsh.

Watercolor.

Rough Going

1981
Bob painted what he felt
some of the first travelers
would have seen as
they crossed the
Animas Forks area.

Tempera- India ink resist.

Telluride

1980s
This building still stands in
Telluride and the lettering
is still visible.

Watercolor.

Red Mountain Gold

1980s
Bob especially likes the
design of the snow on
Red Mountain.

Watercolor.

Continental Divide

1980s
These gold seekers are
on the Continental Divide
as the sun comes up.

Watercolor.

Before Dawn

1980s
Silverton packers are
getting their loads
together before dawn. It's
a long way to the mine.

Watercolor.

Desert Storm

1980s
The storm has just passed as the freighter and a horseman are traveling between Montrose and Grand Junction.

Watercolor.

Dolores to Rico Stage

1980s
Two cowboys wait for
the stage for a ride
to town on a cold
winter day.

Watercolor.

1990s

1990s
Not all of Bob's works
are of a historic nature.
He has also done some
beautiful landscapes.

Watercolor.

Detis at Ophir

1990
Mark Detis had a saloon
at Ophir with a boarding
house on the second
floor. The saloon had a
player piano that took
nickels. Three shifts slept
here – round the clock.

Watercolor.

The Big Muddy

1990s
A lone rider travels
through a thick forest
near McClure Pass.

Watercolor.

The Collin Ranch

1990
This scene off the Last
Dollar Road was
commissioned as a
wedding present.

Oil.

Threshing Crew

1990s
This was a typical scene on Howard's Flat off Dallas Divide about 1900. There were many small farms raising grains.

Watercolor.

Pete DeCamillo

1990s
Pete is still living and
farms a little. Here he is
in his fields with his
irrigating shovel.

Watercolor.

The Gold Guards

1990s
The guards that often traveled with the gold wagons didn't ride alongside. They were usually in the nearby hills scouting for trouble.

Watercolor.

Trout Lake

1995
Ted Nelson of the
Red Barn Restaurant
commissioned this
work. He just liked
Trout Lake. He got his
money's worth.

Watercolor.

Where Avalanches Roll

1990s
Bob meant for this
scene to show just how
vast and enormous
the mountains are
in the San Juans.

Watercolor.

1990
Bob has prospectors
exploring a newly
discovered vein, yet the
gold in the barren rock
is also very evident.

Watercolor.

The Ophir Miners

1990s
The "looseness" of
Bob's present technique
shows through in this
winter painting.

Watercolor.

Bucking Horse

1990s
Another small (8" by 10")
painting that leaves a lot
to the imagination.

Watercolor.

Basque Herder

1990s
This small (8" by 10")
painting of one of Martin
Echardt's sheepherders
was done very quickly
from memory.

Watercolor.

Ore Wagon at Eureka

1990s
In this small (8" by 10")
watercolor the view
would be looking back
towards Silverton.

Watercolor.

1990s
The first rays of the sun
strike this famous peak
near Telluride.

Watercolor.

1990s
Bob painted this scene
for the Fellin brothers
who brought ore
down from the Camp
Bird Mine through the
Waterhole Slide.

Watercolor.

The Ore Handlers

1990s
Bob likes the way the
early morning shadows
come out in this scene
from Creede.

Watercolor.

Brown Station

Storm Clouds

1999
Another example of
Bob's "loose" technique
shows in the sky
behind the Montrose to
Grand Junction stage.

Watercolor.

Sound Democrat Mill Restored

1996
The BLM and volunteers
have restored this mill
near Animas Forks, yet it
still looks old.

Watercolor.

Million Dollar Highway

1994
The scene is very
recognizable today,
but you won't see
the stagecoach on
the highway.

Watercolor.

2000s

Ouray Springs

2000
This scene would have been at the north end of town near where the hot springs pool is today.

Watercolor.

Telluride Depot

2000
The arrival of the
Rio Grande Southern
Railroad meant real
prosperity for Telluride.

Watercolor.

2000
The snows can get deep
in the San Juans. These
men are going to ride
the horses back to town
and abandon the stage.

Watercolor.

Suffolk Transfer House

2000
Ophir Pass is in the
background, while
the skeleton frame
for the tram is behind
the packer.

Watercolor.

Telluride

2000
Another small landscape concentrates on Ajax and other mountains that loom over Telluride.

Watercolor.

Hauling Water, Howard Flats

2000
This is a smaller version of a larger painting that Bob did earlier.

Watercolor.

Freighter

2000
Bob has a "stash" of tempera resist paper as it is not made any more so he paints small in this medium.

Tempera- India ink resist.

Untitled

2000
Bob caught the intense
light and wind
that accompanies a
mountain thunderstorm.

Watercolor.

Ironton Park

2000
Once again Bob really
likes the color and the
"looseness" of this
painting.

Watercolor.

2000
This small painting
caught the sunset
on Sheep Mountain
which looms above
Trout Lake near Telluride.

Watercolor.

Set the Brakes

2000
It was much more difficult for a team to go down hill than up because of the weight of the wagon pushing behind them.

Watercolor.

2000
Bob pointed out that it
was a real challenge for a
watercolorist to capture
the marbling on the wall.

Watercolor.

Cliff Dwellings

The Packers

2000
Loading an animal was
a real art, usually
requiring the coordination
of two men.

Tempera- India ink resist.

Ouray Stage

2000
Once again Bob uses warm colors – this time to show the warmth of the rising sun.

Tempera- India ink resist.

Rio Grande Southern at Fall Creek

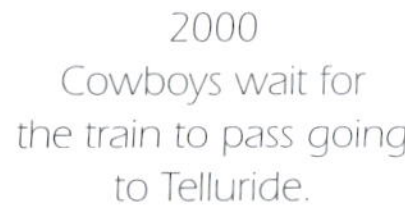

2000
Cowboys wait for
the train to pass going
to Telluride.

Watercolor.

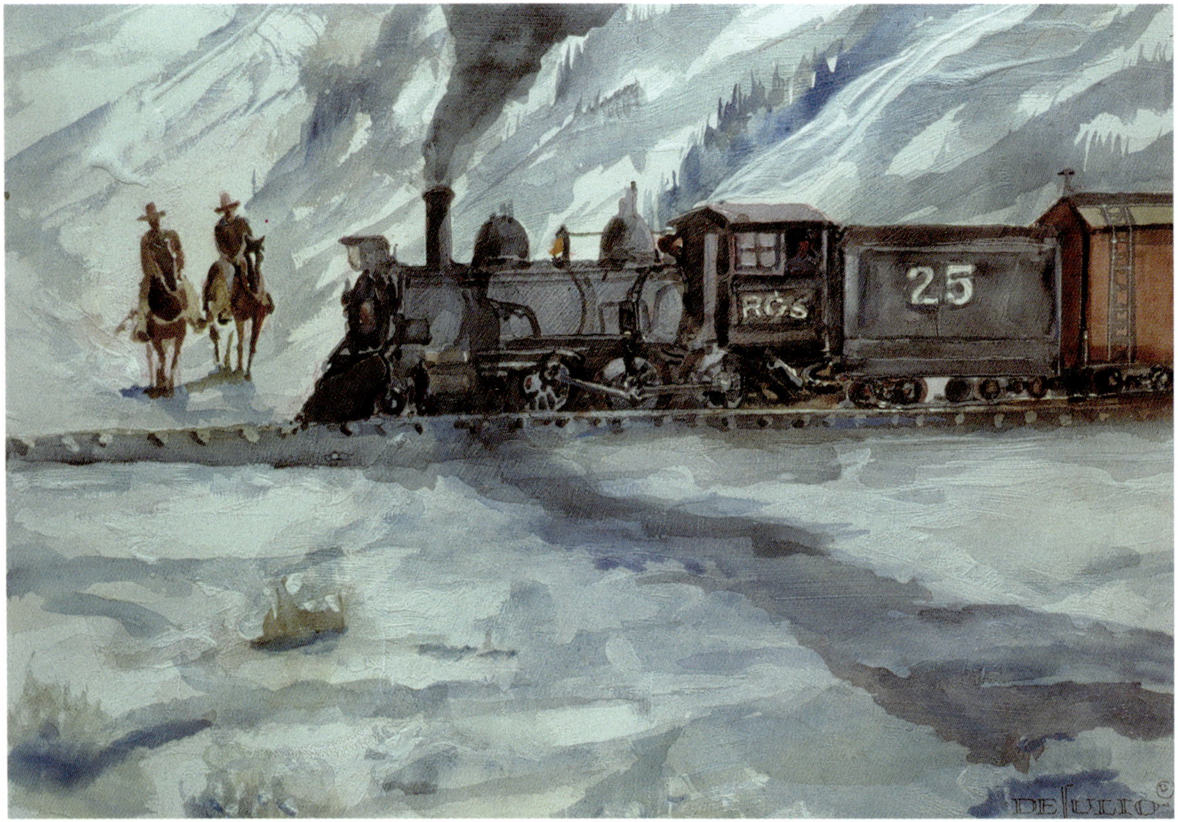

Small Freight Wagon Above Timberline

2000
Bob especially likes the
way the horses came out
in this small painting.

Watercolor.

Sams Colorado

2000
Bob's cousin Carl DeJulio
used to bring his milk
to this small stage stop
(later railroad stop) near
Dallas Divide.

Watercolor.

Telluride Packers

2001
Mules are being loaded
with supplies for the
mines – they were a
vital lifeline.

Watercolor.

2000
Two of Ralph Lauren's cowboys check out this famous home on Dallas Divide.

Watercolor.

2000
These cowboys roll
their own cigarettes.

Watercolor.

Homewood Ranch

WILSON MESA

2001
Bob painted this 100
year-old barn on
commission. It was
built really solid to carry
the snowload.

Watermedia marble.

2001
The wagons are in front
of a thrashing machine
near Montrose that was
powered by the belt
running to a tractor.

Watercolor.

The Remount

2001
This is a Pony Express
stop and the rider is
getting a fresh horse
in a hurry.

Watercolor.

2001
Bob went with Martin
to Howard Flats in
October and after the
leaves were off the trees.

Watercolor.

Old Hundred Mine

2000
This famous mine
sits 2,000 feet above
the valley floor off Stony
Pass. Its boardinghouse is
in the background.

Watercolor.

Lewis Mine

2001
Bob was commissioned by the BLM to document the well preserved Lewis Mine and Mill above Telluride in 2001.
The two upper watercolors (*Lewis Mine Office* on the left and *Lewis Mill* on the right) show how Bob imagined the place almost 100 years ago.
The bottom painting (*The Lewis Mine*) shows the mill today. He did all the paintings from photographs.
The series shows what Bob excels at – seeing the past and the present when he looks at a scene.

Upper – Watercolor.
Lower – Tempera-India ink resist.